THE CHANGING FACE OF
RUSSIA

Text by GALYA RANSOME
Photographs by BOB SMITH

HODDER
Wayland

an imprint of Hodder Children's Books

© 2003 White-Thomson Publishing Ltd

Produced for Hodder Wayland by
White-Thomson Publishing Ltd
2/3 St Andrew's Place
Lewes BN7 1UP

Editor: Kay Barnham/Stephen White-Thomson
Designer: Clare Nicholas
Proofreader: Alison Cooper
Additional picture research: Shelley Noronha, Glass Onion Pictures

First published in Great Britain in 2003 by Hodder Wayland, an imprint of
Hodder Children's Books

British Library Cataloguing in Publication Data
Ransome, Galya
   The Changing Face of Russia
   1. Russia (Federation) - Juvenile literature
   I. Title II. Russia
   947

ISBN 0 7502 3289 7

Printed in Hong Kong

Hodder Children's Books
A division of Hodder Headline Limited
338 Euston Road, London NW1 3BH

Acknowledgements
The publishers would like to thank
the following for their contributions
to this book: Rob Bowden – statistics
research; Peter Bull – map
illustration; Nick Hawken – statistics
panel illustrations. All photographs
are by Bob Smith except: Corbis 14;
Eye Ubiquitous 10; Hodder Wayland
Picture Library 9, 10, 14, 24, 27, 34,
40, 41; Impact Photos 21;
Popperfoto 6, 20, 44

Contents

1 St Petersburg: Northern Capital

The city of St Petersburg was founded by the Russian Tsar Peter the Great in 1703 and was the capital of the Russian Empire until 1918. It is the second-largest Russian city, after Moscow, the largest seaport and home to nearly five million people. St Petersburg is still known as the 'northern capital'.

St Petersburg's history

During its history, St Petersburg has seen many of the dramatic changes that have happened to Russia. In 1917, the Bolshevik Revolution began here, when an armed uprising put the communist party into power. The Bolsheviks murdered the tsar and his family, before taking over the country in the name of its citizens and forming the Soviet Union. In 1924, the city was renamed Leningrad, after Lenin – the leader of the Revolution. During the Second World War, the people of Leningrad were surrounded by the Nazi army and survived a devastating two-year siege – an event that helped to defeat Hitler. After the Soviet Union collapsed in 1991, St Petersburg's citizens voted for the city to return to its old name.

Changes in St Petersburg

In the 1990s, St Petersburg became run down because of a lack of money. Now that the situation has improved, buildings are being renovated or converted into shops and offices. Business and industry are beginning to grow. The city has gone through some difficult times, but it is adapting fast to life after communism. Both Russia and St Petersburg are looking forward to the future.

▲ The eighteenth-century Catherine Palace in Tsarskoye Selo, near St Petersburg, one of the many palaces built for the Russian royal family.

◀ Traffic on Nevsky Prospekt, the main street of St Petersburg. Traffic is a growing problem for many Russian cities.

▲ This map shows the main geographical features of Russia, as well as places mentioned in this book.

RUSSIA: KEY FACTS

Area: 17,075,400 sq km

Population: 145 million

Population density: 8.5 persons per sq km

Capital city: Moscow (8.4 million)

Other main cities (municipalities): St Petersburg (4.7 million); Novosibirsk (1.4 million); Ekaterinburg (1.3 million); Samara (1.2 million)

Highest mountain: El'brus, Caucasus (5,642 m)

Longest river: Lena (4,320 km)

Main language: Russian

Major religions: Christianity (Russian Orthodox Church); Islam. No percentage data available.

Currency: rouble (1 rouble = 100 kopeks)

Past Times

In 1917, the Russian Empire, which covered a sixth of the world's land surface, became the world's first communist state. Known as the Soviet Union (or USSR), it was made up of fifteen countries called republics.

Under communist rule

Between 1917 and 1991 the Soviet government controlled everything. All agricultural land was organized into large collective farms, where everyone worked for the state and all produce was sold by the state. Huge factories were built to supply the whole Soviet Union. The needs of ordinary people were neglected, while priority was given to developing military and space technology. Freedom and choice were limited and the standard of living was low.

In 1985, Mikhail Gorbachev became Soviet leader. Realizing the need for reform, he launched the policies of *perestroika* (restructuring the economic and political systems) and *glasnost* (openness). Gorbachev's reforms quickly led to the collapse of the Soviet Union and the end of the communist party's rule.

▲ *Lenin's mausoleum on Red Square in Moscow where the mummified body of Lenin is still visited by thousands of people every year.*

◀ *The US president Reagan and the Soviet leader Gorbachev during one of their meetings. Gorbachev was the Soviet president most liked by Western leaders. He started* perestroika *and* glasnost *and was the last leader of the Soviet Union.*

The end of communism

In 1991, Russia and the other Soviet republics became
independent. Boris Yeltsin was Russia's first democratically
elected president – it was his job to reorganize the country.
As the communist system collapsed, inflation soared and
crime increased. In 1999,
Vladimir Putin became
the Russian president.
His aims were to tackle
corruption and crime and
to re-establish Russia as a
major world power.

► *Commercial advertising of
this type was not allowed in
the Soviet Union. Today there
is as much advertising in
Russia as in the West.*

IN THEIR OWN WORDS

'My name is Svetlana Andreyevna Serova and I
am a schoolteacher. My parents lived before
perestroika, when life was very different and easier
in some ways than today. Many things have
changed since 1991. Although there are more
opportunities for young people life is more
difficult for older people. People can travel
abroad and see foreign countries but the majority
of people can't afford it. We have to pay for
medical care – for some people, this is very
difficult. Our culture is changing too. In the past,
there was censorship and films seemed to be
better. Now they show bad programmes on TV
and there are too many advertisements. I think
we need more Russian traditions and more
Russian music.'

Landscape and Climate

Russia is the largest country in the world, covering more than one-ninth of the world's land surface. It is seventy times larger than the UK, nearly twice as big as the USA, and spans eleven time zones. It shares borders with many countries, including Finland, Kazakhstan, Mongolia and China.

Coasts, rivers and lakes

Russia has the longest coastline of any country – it stretches 37,350 km, mainly along the Arctic and Pacific Oceans. Most of the major rivers flow into the Arctic Ocean and are frozen for up to eight months a year. The River Lena is the longest, at 4,320 km. The Ob and Irtysh form one of the largest river systems in the world.

The Volga (3,530 km), which flows into the Caspian Sea, is the longest river in Europe. It has great importance for Russia, because of the many giant dams and hydroelectric power stations that have been built across it. The Caspian Sea is the world's largest salt-water lake. It covers 386,400 square km – an area bigger than Japan – and is 1,000 km long.

▲ Lake Ladoga, the largest lake in Europe, is part of a canal system linking the Baltic and White Seas.

◀ The Moscow River flows through the Russian capital, past the Kremlin, on its way towards the Volga, the longest river in Europe.

IN THEIR OWN WORDS

'My name is Ulyana Lavrentyeva. I live in Akademgorodok in Siberia outside the city of Novosibirsk. Winters in Siberia are cold but in summer it is hot. Summers could be nice if it wasn't for mosquitoes. They can be quite vicious! We live on the border between the taiga and the steppe. We can either go to pick mushrooms in the forest or visit lakes in the steppe. We also have a big artificial lake near our city, created when a dam was built across the river Ob. It is beautiful there, but the shoreline is slowly being eaten away by the water, which is very sad.'

The Caspian Sea is rich in oil but its ownership is at present disputed between Russia and the other countries on its shores.

Another record-breaking Russian lake is Lake Baikal in Siberia, which is the deepest freshwater lake in the world. It has a maximum depth of 1,620 m and is home to thousands of animal species, including the rare freshwater seal.

▼ Russia has thousands of lakes, with great natural beauty and well stocked with fish.

Mountains and plains

The Ural Mountains divide the huge, flat plain that stretches across Russia, and the Caucasus Mountains are located in the south-west, between the Black Sea and the Caspian Sea. The highest peak in the Caucasus Mountains is an extinct volcano called El'brus (5,642 m), which is also the highest point in Europe.

◀ *The Ural Mountains divide Europe and Asia. They stretch from the Arctic Ocean to the Caspian Sea.*

Forests and tundra

Nearly a quarter of the world's woodlands are in Russia. Forest covers much of the northern part of Russia and Siberia, where it is known as taiga. In the far north of Siberia is tundra – a bitterly cold, treeless area where very few people live. The soil beneath the surface is called permafrost, as it is permanently frozen. The tundra has many mineral resources, including oil and natural gas.

▼ *The Siberian taiga is a coniferous forested region that lies south of the treeless arctic tundra. It occupies two-fifths of European Russia and covers much of Siberia.*

Climate

Russia has a harsh climate that suffers from extremes of temperature. In general, winters are long and cold, while summers are short and hot – although it is colder in the north and warmer in the south. The north of Siberia is the coldest inhabited place in the world – temperatures can reach as low as -70°C – whereas in the south, temperatures can reach 40°C. In central Russia, winters are bearably cold, but summers are pleasantly hot. In recent years, there have been climate changes, which may be because of global warming. For example, it is now quite common for snow to fall and melt several times during the winter, whereas in the past it would have remained frozen throughout.

▲ *Annual rainfall decreases from west to east across Russia, but is a fact of life in all the major cities of European Russia.*

IN THEIR OWN WORDS

'My name is Ekaterina Nilovna Gromova. I am a retired engineer. I worked for many years in Murmansk in the Kola peninsula. Murmansk is the largest city and port inside the Arctic Circle. The sea never freezes there. The Murmansk region lies in two geographical zones – tundra and taiga. There are no trees in the tundra, so there is nothing to break the high winds. Winters are very cold there. Summer lasts for only 60 days and we have even had snow in August.'

4

Natural Resources

Russia has more natural resources than any other country in the world. The major oil deposits are in western and eastern Siberia and the Volga–Ural region. Nearly half of the world's coal reserves are in Russia, with the largest coalfields in central and eastern Siberia. Although the country has the world's largest deposits of mineral resources, many of these are difficult to extract because they are in remote areas with extreme weather conditions. Transportation from these remote areas is another big problem because there are often no roads or railways near the resources.

▲ *The River Volga is a key transportation route in European Russia. Barges have always been used to transport heavy goods along this river and still play an important role in the Russian distribution system today.*

Russia's energy supply

Many rivers run hydroelectric power stations, which produce nearly 20 per cent of all Russia's electricity needs. Another 66 per cent of Russian electricity comes from fossil fuel and the remaining 14 per cent from nuclear power. It is planned to expand the nuclear industry to power 25 per cent of the home market by 2020.

▶ *One of the 'wedding cake' buildings in Moscow, constructed during the communist leader Stalin's rule. These huge buildings are floodlit at night, making a magnificent sight, but using a lot of electricity.*

Gas

Russia is fortunate enough to own about 40 per cent of the world's reserves of natural gas. A large amount is sold to Western Europe. The Russian gas sector is dominated by a company called Gazprom, which is partly owned by the Russian government. Gazprom produces the vast majority of the country's natural gas and also controls Russia's pipeline network. However, despite large deposits, domestic gas prices are rising.

▲ *The Gazprom headquarters in Moscow. Gazprom is Russia's main energy supplier and earns much foreign currency with its gas exports.*

IN THEIR OWN WORDS

'My name is Artyom Vitalyevich. I live in Moscow and I work for Gazprom – one of the largest gas companies in the world. About 20 per cent of the world's gas is provided by our company, which has the longest gas pipeline in the world and is one of the largest employers in the country. We supply gas to several countries abroad and are planning to extend our pipelines and increase our sales. Exports of gas are very important for the Russian economy. We are also investing a lot of money in ecological projects to make sure that no further damage is done to the environment.'

Oil

Oil production is very important for Russia – it provides about a quarter of the government's income and employs thousands of people. The main Russian oil company, Transneft, is the largest oil transporting company in the world. The overall length of its pipeline is 46,800 km. This is longer than the length of the Equator.

As the second-largest oil exporter in the world after Saudi Arabia, Russia supplies about one-eighth of the world's oil. This is sold to many European countries, including the UK, France, Germany, Italy and Spain. Many oil deposits have yet to be developed, so it is estimated that Russia's oil reserves will last for well over fifty years.

▲ *The Trans-Siberian oil pipeline stretches thousands of kilometres through difficult and hostile landscape. There were many problems to overcome during its construction and it requires constant maintenance.*

◄ *Russia is the world's second-largest oil producer and exports a large part of its crude oil production. Large refineries also supply the growing domestic market.*

Forestry

About a quarter of the world's forests are in Russia. However, Russia produces only 3 per cent of the world's timber, as the forests are often in very inaccessible areas of the country. Usually, the country exports unfinished lumber and then imports finished wood at a much higher price. At present, anybody can lease a forest for a period of five years. The government wants to grant licences for up to forty-nine years.

IN THEIR OWN WORDS

'My name is Katya Bochkova. I am 22. As a student I took part in folklore expeditions. We travelled to the northern city of Archangel. I was amazed by the vastness of the forest there. When you fly over the taiga it seems it has no end – just a huge green expanse of forest. You can mainly see birch trees outside Moscow but the taiga forest is very different – it is so thick and unspoiled. There are so many animals including bears, foxes and deer. I didn't see any bears but I saw foxes and deer. I was also amazed to meet many professional hunters. They hunted animals and sold their furs. I had not imagined that people earned their living this way.'

These longer licences will encourage investment and the building of factories so that timber can be processed and finished in Russia, rather than abroad.

On the other hand, deforestation is a big issue for Russia. Thousands of hectares of forests disappear each year. Some Russian experts believe that the forests will re-grow naturally. However, ecologists believe that the rapid cutting of forests will lead to climate change.

▼ The forests of central Russia are different from the taiga. The birch tree is a national Russian symbol.

Renewable energy

Since the country has such abundant fossil fuels, so far little attention has been paid to alternative energy sources like wind or solar power. At the moment there are no plans for future development.

5

The Changing Environment

While the communists were in power every effort was made to improve industry and produce enough food for the Soviet Union's own people, and large amounts of money were spent on developing and producing weapons. Meanwhile, very little attention was paid to the environment – industrial waste, fertilizers, pesticides and untreated sewage flowed into rivers and lakes. Also, industry pumped carbon dioxide and other harmful substances into the atmosphere. Many years of neglect turned Russia into one of the most polluted countries in the world, affecting the environment and the health of people, animals and plants. However, there are at last plans for a proper environmental policy to be developed.

▼ *Russia has more than 600 thermal power stations that use mainly gas. They join the rest of industry in being a polluter of the environment. However, cars remain the main cause of urban pollution.*

Air pollution

The Soviet Union was the world's main air polluter. Ecologists believed it to be the main contributor to global warming. Thanks mainly to the reduction in industrial output since the collapse of the Soviet Union, the situation is now improving.

IN THEIR OWN WORDS

'My name is Pavel and I am a biologist. As a young person, I am concerned about the cleanliness of the air that we breathe and the water we drink. In St Petersburg the air is very polluted. I have heard that Greenpeace has been campaigning in Russia since 1992, for example, against the cutting of forests in Karelia. It is very hard to fight against the big companies and the government, but I am glad that someone cares enough to try to do so. It was partly due to Greenpeace that places like Lake Baikal were made World Heritage Sites – sites of world importance.'

The effects of Russia's industry mean that in some cities air pollution is up to ten times higher than the permitted level. Although air pollution in Moscow is less than in some other Russian cities, it is still about four times higher than it should be. In Soviet times, the government tried to move industry out of the capital, but there was not enough money to build new factories elsewhere. Recently, measures have been taken to cut down on pollution in Moscow. Several factories have been closed and a local oil refinery has been ordered to stop burning off unwanted gas.

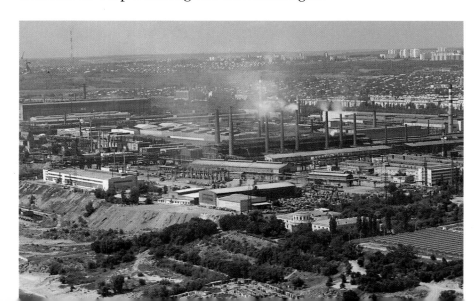

◄ Many factories closed down after the collapse of the Soviet Union. However, industrial pollution in big cities is still a problem.

Car pollution

In the Soviet Union, it was very difficult to buy a car – there was a long waiting list and prices were kept artificially high by the state. Today, there are no waiting lists, private companies sell cars and many people can afford to buy them. As well as nearly two million cars in Moscow, about 200,000 vehicles drive into the city every day. The downside is that vehicles are currently the main air polluters in Russia. Car exhaust gases are responsible for 87 per cent of all air pollution.

In 1997, along with most of the world's countries, Russia signed the Kyoto agreement. Its aim was to reduce greenhouse-gas emissions around the world by setting each country a pollution-reduction target. It is hoped that Russia will meet its target.

▲ *There are quite a few old vehicles on Russian roads that pollute the air. Trams are much friendlier to the environment.*

Water pollution

Industrial pollution affects not only the air, but also the quality of drinking water in Russia. Rivers and seas are polluted when industrial waste is discharged directly

◄ *River pollution caused by many years of neglect of the environment during the Soviet period.*

◄ *Much of the Russian coastline has been polluted with industrial waste. Little money is spent on environmental care or protection.*

into waterways. The Soviet authorities made little effort to regulate factories. In Russia too there are many examples of serious damage still being done to water quality. Even Lake Baikal has been affected. A further threat to water quality comes from old nuclear submarines that have been dumped on the northern coasts of Russia.

IN THEIR OWN WORDS

'My name is Lubov Semyonovna and I live in St Petersburg. I am an administrator in the local government offices. Car pollution seems to be a big problem in our city. In the early 1990s, when many factories closed, the air was very clean. Even today, there are not many big factories that pollute the air. The main culprits are the cars on the road. Everybody complains about how hard life is, but the number of private cars has increased considerably in the last ten years. The roads are very congested. It seems to me that car pollution is getting worse every day.'

Nuclear pollution

From the 1940s onwards, the nuclear weapons and power industries were priorities for the Soviet government. There are huge stockpiles of nuclear waste in Russia – possibly as much as 200 million tonnes. When a nuclear reactor exploded at the Chernobyl nuclear energy plant in 1986, it polluted a large area of Europe – as far west as Wales. There have been other serious incidents at nuclear plants, for example, at Chelyabinsk in 1957, when the cooling system of a radioactive waste containment unit went wrong and exploded.

Russia spent years building a huge underground nuclear reprocessing plant at Krasnoyarsk in Siberia. They hope to clear the backlog of nuclear waste and will also reprocess waste from other countries. The Duma – the Russian parliament – has ruled that any income from Krasnoyarsk will be used for projects to improve the environment.

▲ *In 1954 the Obninsk nuclear power plant was the first in the world to produce electricity. Today there are more than 50 nuclear power plants working in Russia.*

Ecology

More and more Russians are becoming aware of ecology – the study of living things and their environment. Since 1991, several ecological pressure groups have been founded. Thanks to their efforts, some positive changes have taken place in recent years. Lake Baikal, for example, has become a World Heritage Site, considered by the United Nations to be a site of great importance for the natural heritage of the world.

Recycling and waste

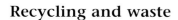

Western-style packaging is becoming more popular and produces a lot more waste. At the moment, Russian society does not recycle much waste, which could become a problem if it is not encouraged more in the future.

▲ *Russian winters are very cold. Even Lake Baikal freezes over, in spite of being the deepest freshwater lake in the world. A unique variety of plant and animal life is found in its clear waters.*

IN THEIR OWN WORDS

'My name is Larissa and I am a 32-year-old psychologist. I am interested in ecology because it affects our health and our lives. I live in Voronezh. We have a big nuclear power station just outside our city. They were going to build another one, but the Chernobyl disaster made people more aware of the problems of nuclear power. Local people protested against the new station and the plans were scrapped. I think it was the right decision. I'm not sure what the alternative should be. Maybe we should use more hydroelectric power or more solar or wind power, but I am definitely against more nuclear power stations being built.'

6 The Changing Population

Russia is the world's largest country, and population density in some regions is the lowest in the world. In northern parts of Russia, an average of just one person lives in each square kilometre, compared to about nine people per square kilometre across the country as a whole. The majority of Russians live in the European part of the country, where about 25 people live in each square kilometre. By comparison, the Moscow region is very crowded, with more than 300 people per square kilometre.

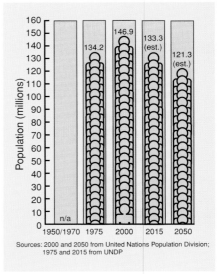

Sources: 2000 and 2050 from United Nations Population Division; 1975 and 2015 from UNDP

▲ The Russian government is concerned that the country's population is predicted to decline sharply.

◄ New markets and shopping centres are opening up all over Russia. Although the overall population of Russia is shrinking, the numbers living in towns are growing. Population density in Moscow is particularly high.

Population decline

A major concern for the Russian government, which wants the country to develop and prosper, is population decline. The birth rate has been slowly decreasing for several decades and in 1992, for the first time, more Russians died than were born. In 2001, the population fell by 0.35 per cent – over half a million people.

◄ *Many young Russians are not in a hurry to start a family, so this young couple is quite exceptional in becoming young parents.*

There are several reasons for the shrinking population. The Russian birth rate is very low – in 2001, the average number of children per family was just 1.3. The greater opportunities now on offer to Russians mean that some women are choosing to develop their careers or enjoy foreign holidays before having children. Another problem is the high death rate among infants, due to poor healthcare in maternity hospitals. More young people are dying because of alcohol and drug abuse. Life expectancy has dropped since 1991. On average, men can expect to live until they are 59 years old (6 years less than in 1991), while women's life expectancy is down from 74 to 72 years.

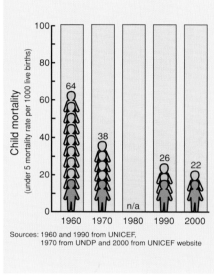

Child mortality (under 5 mortality rate per 1000 live births)

	1960	1970	1980	1990	2000
	64	38	n/a	26	22

Sources: 1960 and 1990 from UNICEF, 1970 from UNDP and 2000 from UNICEF website

▲ *The mortality rate amongst children under 5 is dropping, but is still too high.*

IN THEIR OWN WORDS

'My name is Aza Hazbulatova. I am 29 and am from Ingushetia, in the south of Russia, next to Chechnya. I came to Moscow five years ago to live with my brother's family. Moscow is fantastic and I would like to stay here. There are many job opportunities here, and lots of new businesses. I work in a travel agency and tourism is flourishing. I would eventually like to have two children, which is more than most families have these days, but I will wait until I am married before starting a family.'

Immigration and emigration

If people with Russian nationality were not returning to Russia from former Soviet republics, the population decline would be even more serious. During Soviet times, Russian was the official language – all Soviet citizens studied it and spoke it quite well. However, Russians who had moved to the smaller republics did not usually speak the language of the republic they were living in. There was no need for it.

In 1991, after the Soviet Union broke up and its republics became independent, each country insisted on its own national language becoming the official language. Many Russians became foreigners in these new countries. Language difficulties meant that some people could not find work and so returned to Russia. The influx of people has put pressure on housing and social services in some parts of Russia, especially in Moscow.

A diverse population

On 1 December 2001, there were 145 million people in Russia. Among them are 120 million Russians, 5.5 million Tatars, 4.4 million Ukrainians, 1.8 million Chuvashi and over eighty other ethnic groups that inhabit Russia's huge territory. The government in the Soviet

▼ *Takhir from Tadzhikistan selling dried fruit, nuts and fish at the market in Moscow.*

IN THEIR OWN WORDS

'My name is Roman Tutsuda and I am an archpriest in the Orthodox Church. Since 1988, when religion was permitted, the authorities have stopped interfering in church affairs. Today, many young people go to church and several Orthodox schools have been founded. Priests are also allowed to visit schools, hospitals and military units to talk with people there. The Church is becoming more active in the life of Russia. Our main concern is the spiritual – the inner world of a person. But, we have only had a few years of freedom, to make up for over seventy years of oppression, and there is still much to do.'

Union did not approve of religion. But now, amongst this diverse population, different faiths, such as Islam, are growing. Orthodox Christianity, the main religion in Russia, survived communism and is now enjoying a period of growth.

◄ The Cathedral of Christ the Saviour, rebuilt in the late 1990s after being demolished by communists in the 1930s. Many new places of worship have been opened by the Russian Orthodox Church since the collapse of the Soviet Union.

7 Changes at Home

The collapse of the Soviet system has brought more opportunities and choice for Russian people, but has also changed the balance in some households. In the past, the man was considered to be the head of the family, but many Russian women now earn as much as, or more than, their husbands. This may take some getting used to.

Young people

Today, young Russian people are not in a hurry to start a family. First, they want to see the world or develop a career. They have opportunities that their parents could only dream of. Living standards are rising, foreign travel is easier, shops have more choice and career opportunities are much more exciting.

Most of the Soviet youth organizations that used to occupy young people in their spare time and during holidays are gone. Instead, there are discos and clubs. A lot of young people now have part-time jobs to earn enough money to pay for their lifestyle.

▼ Young people in post-Soviet Russia now enjoy the same pastimes, music and fashions as their counterparts in the West.

IN THEIR OWN WORDS

'My name is Natasha and I am 24. I was born in the Perm region near the Ural Mountains, but came to Moscow to study in the Chemical Institute. I have a degree in chemistry, but an engineer's salary is very small – it is impossible to survive on it. I earn more by selling souvenirs. I think it was easier for our parents – their homes were given to them by the state. Today, you have to work all your life to earn enough money for even a very small flat. In the future, I would like to train and work as a make-up artist, and have a family.'

◀ *Many shops stock luxury goods for rich 'New Russians' to buy.*

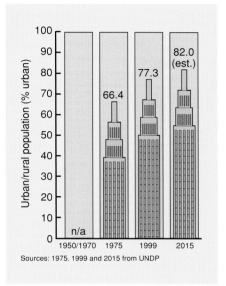

▲ *Russia is rapidly becoming a much more urban society.*

The 'New Russians'

People are now allowed to own property – in the past the state owned everything – and many are buying houses and flats. During the first years after communism, some people became rich very quickly and have become known as 'New Russians'. They are not popular with ordinary Russians. Most people would agree that their life is better than in Soviet times, but feel there is great pressure on them to earn enough to pay for it.

▼ *A lot of expensive* dachas, *or summer country houses, have been built in recent years. A new generation of successful Russian entrepreneurs and business people can afford houses like this one.*

Education

In Soviet Russia, education was free, but was totally controlled by the state. All schools had the same curriculum and textbooks, and all subjects were compulsory.
Nearly 70 per cent of Soviet children went to nurseries or kindergartens that were partly paid for by the state. After 1991, the state nursery sector quickly disappeared. Parents had to make other arrangements – they could pay for private nurseries or ask family members to help. Today, the majority of schools and educational establishments need modernization and new facilities. More than half of all parents have to contribute towards their children's education.

Changes have also been made to the curriculum. Textbooks on history, politics, religion and the economy – written from the Soviet point of view – have been updated. Older pupils can now choose which subjects to study, but there is often a shortage of teachers, especially for new subjects, such as Information Technology.

▲ Many Russian children are looked after by their grandmothers. The Soviet Union provided subsidized nursery schools for all children, but these have largely disappeared from modern Russia.

◄ Teaching is still a largely female profession.

IN THEIR OWN WORDS

'My name is Nadezhda Anatolyevna and I live in Tver. This is a large town on the main road from Moscow to St Petersburg. I am a grandmother – I have a son, a daughter and three grandchildren. Today, I'm looking after my 19-month-old granddaughter. I used to work in a bakery, but I retired two years ago. It's just as well I'm not working. There are no state nurseries any more and private childcare is very expensive. Grandmothers have to help their children any way they can, so I take care of my grandchildren while my children go to work.'

Private schools now exist, but the vast majority of pupils still go to state schools. A small percentage of children, especially those of well-off parents, are sent to study in boarding schools abroad. Many go to the UK or USA.

Higher education

Over half of university students pay for their education – the most popular subjects are economics and accountancy. At present universities set their own entrance examinations. However, there are plans to introduce a single examination that will give all pupils the chance to apply to the university of their choice. This will reduce corruption in university entrance procedures.

▶ *Moscow State University is one of the oldest universities in Russia. It was founded in 1755.*

The armed forces

In Russia, national service in the armed forces is compulsory for 18-year-old men, although many try to avoid this with bogus health certificates. The Chechen conflict in the south of Russia and difficult living conditions for soldiers have made military service even more unpopular. The government is now trying to introduce alternative service – work in the community – for those whose beliefs do not allow them to carry out military service.

Since Soviet times, Russia has halved its armed forces. The country still has about a million conscripted soldiers and professional officers, but this is still too many to clothe and feed. Proposals are being discussed to reduce the army even more, by doing away with national service. Russia is also seeking closer links with NATO, to become more involved in peacekeeping initiatives.

▲ It is prestigious to serve as a guard at the Moscow Kremlin. This is the heart of Russian government and a long way from the troubles in Chechnya in the south.

IN THEIR OWN WORDS

'Our names are Evgeny and Oleg. We're cadets in the Engineering Naval College – we're going to be naval officers and serve in the Russian Northern Fleet. In order to become a naval officer you need to study for five years. This is our first year. So far, we've had to pass exams in maths, physics, Russian and fitness. The Russian fleet is becoming stronger and we are proud that in the future we are going to defend our motherland. In five to ten years, we're sure that everything will be better in Russia.'

Healthcare

Since the early 1990s, a two-tier system of healthcare has developed in Russia. There are many well-staffed private hospitals with the latest technology, but state hospitals are usually short of medicines and modern equipment, because the state cannot afford to fund them properly.

A healthcare insurance system, paid for with contributions from people's salaries, was introduced in 1993, but the money collected is not enough to cover the costs of the health service. Consultations with the family doctor remain free, but people usually have to pay for treatment.

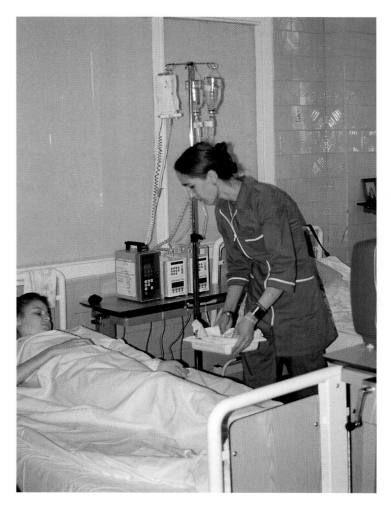

▶ *Some Russian hospitals are doing better than others. This hospital for sick children has good modern equipment and is one of the best in St Petersburg.*

Food and shopping

When Russia was part of the Soviet Union, most people were not able to buy oranges or bananas. Shops sold basic food and consumer goods, but choice was limited. People might have to queue for several hours to buy essentials, like potatoes, sugar or bread. Since then, there have been great changes in shopping in Russia. In bigger towns, there are many more supermarkets and shopping centres, and a range of items on sale that could only have been dreamt of in Soviet times – like Rolex watches and the most expensive French perfumes.

At the beginning of the 1990s, the government used oil revenue to buy large amounts of foreign goods and food – anything foreign was very popular. Today things have changed. Shopping for food and other goods is so much easier – there are no queues and shops are well stocked. People have more confidence in Russian-made food and goods because the quality has improved.

Window-shopping is a new hobby in Russia. Recently, expensive designer shops – both foreign and Russian – have opened, but their prices look more like an annual salary for most people!

▲ *There are shops to cater for all tastes. This shopping mall in Moscow has many designer shops.*

▼ *Fast food shops are very popular in Moscow and are opening up all over Russia.*

▲ *Eating out is very popular in Russia today. There are many new cafés and fast food shops where it is possible to have a full meal or just a quick snack.*

Eating out

Western fast-food chains have opened branches all over Russia. Many foreign restaurants appeared in the country at the beginning of the 1990s. Following their examples, similar Russian 'bistros' opened offering fast food Russian recipes. There are now restaurants and eating places to suit any taste and pocket. A restaurant meal was always a popular way for Russians to celebrate and this remains the case today.

IN THEIR OWN WORDS

'We are road sweepers and it is our lunch break now. Some of us have been doing this job for 20 years. We don't like the job but it pays a salary and we can retire at the age of 55. We work from 8 a.m. till 4 p.m. Work is harder now - there is more litter and dirt on the roads. Work is not easier but shopping is much easier today than it was in the past. We used to spend most of our time in queues trying to buy food or shoes or clothes. Today it is very easy. You can buy everything. There are many restaurants, cafés and other places to eat too, but we can only afford to eat out on special occasions.'

Sport

Sport was very important in Soviet times, but there is now less opportunity to take part. State funding of youth organizations has been reduced or has disappeared altogether. Even large towns have few facilities. At the same time, many private – and expensive – health clubs and exclusive leisure centres have opened. They are often in remote areas that are accessible only by car. Although the government is trying to encourage all Russians to take up sport again, it remains to be seen whether they will be successful.

▲ *Students enjoy sport after lectures at Moscow State University. The Russian government wants to encourage young people to do more sport.*

◄ *Football is a very popular spectator sport in Russia, but it is mainly played during summer months. Ice hockey is more popular in winter.*

Leisure

In the Soviet Union, Western pop music was not allowed – the government was afraid that the West would corrupt young citizens' minds. Now, if they want to, young people are free to have the same interests, listen to the same music and follow the same fashions as those living in the West.

Many Russian groups are also very successful – some have enjoyed international chart success. There are plenty of clubs and bars that play music – some are open all day and all night.

The Internet keeps young people up to date with the latest news and developments around the globe. The number of homes with Internet access is growing. Many talented Russian programmers are helping the country's computer industry to develop rapidly – and catch up with the rest of the world.

▶ *She has a long way to go before she can skate properly! Inline skating is quite a rare sport in Russia but it is growing in popularity.*

IN THEIR OWN WORDS

'My name is Tanya. I am a student. I think young people in Russia have the same interests as young people abroad. I like modern music, and going to night-clubs – we have some really good ones with all the latest Russian and Western music. I keep up with the latest music and fashion news on the Internet. My boyfriend is a web designer and programmer. He has a lot of work and is well paid for it. He recently joined a health club but doesn't go there often because it is a long drive out of town. I know I don't exercise enough. I did sport at school but there is nowhere for me to do it near where I live.'

Changes at Work

For over seventy years, life was centrally planned and controlled in the Soviet Union. A government committee decided everything that was to be produced – from nuts and bolts to beetroot. The price of each product was also set centrally. So a spoon, for example, cost exactly the same no matter where it was bought throughout the fifteen Soviet republics.

Officially, there was no inflation and no unemployment and there were no strikes. In reality, much of Soviet industry was inefficient and made poor-quality products. Huge plants and factories producing goods for the whole Soviet Union meant that all regions of the Soviet Union were dependent on each other. When the Soviet Union ceased to exist, the link between the regions was broken and the economy –– the country's money system – collapsed very quickly.

Painful changes

The change from a centrally controlled and planned economy to a 'market economy' – where goods are sold between different areas and prices go up and down according to demand – was neither easy nor quick. There was often no money to pay salaries for several months and some workers were paid with the goods they produced. Many plants and factories had to close and much of manufacturing industry later failed. It was making out-dated and poor-quality goods that could not compete with cheap but better-quality imports.

▲ *Since the collapse of the Soviet Union many private banks have opened up in Russia.*

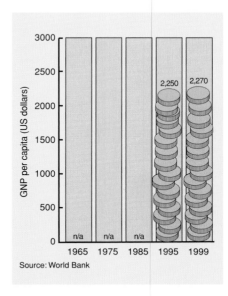

Source: World Bank

▲ *Figures for the national wealth per head of population (per capita), only recently available, show a small rise from 1995 to 1999.*

Freedom of the press

The collapse of the Soviet Union brought big changes in the Russian media. There were many new radio and TV stations and newspapers. A new generation of journalists replaced those of the Soviet era and had more freedom to express their opinions.

▶ *Although very good, the public transport system cannot cope with everyone who needs to make a journey in big cities. Private car owners are often willing to be flagged down and used as unofficial taxis.*

IN THEIR OWN WORDS

'My name is Andrey and I am 29. I studied journalism at Moscow State University. I know that for journalists in Soviet times there were many restrictions and no freedom of speech. However, when I started work, it was a time of opportunities in the Russian media, as many old journalists preferred to leave the profession, rather than adapt. Many new TV channels and newspapers appeared but not all of them survived. Life keeps changing all the time. I don't like all the changes but I look to the future with optimism because I am an optimist by nature.'

The road to recovery

In 1991, the government allowed prices for all goods to be set by the people selling them. Prices rocketed and Russia saw its first strikes for over seventy years as workers protested.

The period between 1989 and 1998 was a very difficult one as industrial production and trade in Russia fell by 44 per cent. However, the economy is slowly recovering. The new market economy aims to produce what people want at prices they can afford. More factories are producing goods needed in everyday life, like food, clothes and items for the home. Information Technology and the service and construction industries are all booming, and unemployment has fallen to 8 per cent of the workforce.

▲ *The harsh Russian climate takes its toll of Russian roads. The recovering economy is now allowing repairs to be more regularly carried out than in the 1990s.*

Private business

In 1991, people were first allowed to start their own companies – one year later, there were nearly 200,000 of them. Now some 35 per cent of the workforce is employed by small businesses rather than the state. Private companies cover all spheres of life: building, industry, agriculture,

◄ *New buildings are going up all over Russia. It is now possible to buy and sell a flat or house, which was not the case in the Soviet Union.*

healthcare and retailing. Consumers now have a choice of who to buy from and companies rely for their future business on customers being satisfied. As a result, both customer service is better and the quality of goods on sale has improved considerably. Whether they are buying meat at the market or hiring a plumber, Russian consumers can now expect proper value for money.

► *The telecommunications revolution has reached Russia too, with many people regularly using mobile phones. New public telephones are also being installed, using up-to-date card payments rather than coins.*

IN THEIR OWN WORDS

'My name is Sasha. This is my wife Sveta and our two-year-old son, Misha. I used to work as a taxi driver and my wife worked as a clerk in a bank. Today, we have our own business. We started selling beer wholesale more than five years ago and our company is now doing quite well. We have a couple of large trucks and employ about ten people. Of course, there is a lot of stress, especially with keeping records of sales and orders, but the more you work the more money you earn. I also like being my own boss. Life is not bad at the moment, but we would prefer to have a clearer tax policy and better pension funds.'

Agriculture

After the collapse of the Soviet Union, agriculture was affected as badly as the rest of the economy. The farms could not cope with the new demands of the market. They did not have enough workers, as many young people left to find jobs in cities. In 1990, a law was passed that allowed people to buy land – six years later, there were nearly 300,000 small farms in Russia. And, unlike the old state-owned farms, these farms could sell for profit and so support themselves.

▼ *Small private farms usually do not have up-to-date machinery. Profits from their production should make it possible from now on for private farmers to invest in modern equipment.*

Farming is developing and improving slowly. More efficient use is being made of the land and the quality of produce is rising. A lack of resources means that Russian farmers tend not to use many chemical fertilizers and pesticides, so vegetables and meat are relatively 'organic'. Russia still has to import some food but is self-sufficient in all the basics.

IN THEIR OWN WORDS

'My name is Michael. I am 63 years old. Two years ago I retired from my job in the factory where I worked for forty years. My pension is not very big and prices have gone up a lot. I work now for this small farm. The work is not easy, all the equipment is old and they don't always pay us on time. Only pensioners work here. The younger generation doesn't want to work on the land any more. The things we produce are good quality and easy enough to sell, so I hope the farm will continue to do well. They are changing the way we pay tax, and I do not suppose that will leave us with any more money in our pockets!'

Paying for Russia's future

A new system of taxation has been a priority for the government. If the Russian government does not collect enough tax to pay for the running of the country, the country will be in serious difficulties. In 2002, a new tax system was introduced. A big publicity campaign was launched to encourage workers to pay tax and ensure that Russia's future is well-funded.

▼ *Typical residential tower blocks. The majority of people in Russia live in flats.*

Women

Women make up more than half of the Russian population and, since the collapse of the Soviet system, life has become more difficult for them in some ways. They are often the first to be made unemployed, as companies are anxious to avoid paying child allowance and maternity leave, which are quite generous in Russia. On the other hand, the changes that have taken place in Russia have also given women opportunities to develop their careers, improve their standard of living and become more independent. Many women have opened new businesses, become managers and directors of companies and even been elected as politicians.

▲ *Some mothers have to stay at home to look after children because free state nurseries are no longer available.*

▲ *Women have new opportunities to start their own business or develop their career. It is increasingly common to see a woman in charge of a company.*

Tourism

In Soviet times, the authorities did not want their citizens to have the freedom to travel abroad. Only a very privileged few, usually communist party members, were allowed out of the country. This changed when Russia became independent. Since then, over 15,000 tourist agencies have opened, organizing trips to places all over the world – and business is booming. The improving economy also means that many

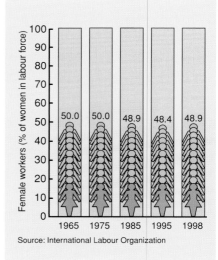

Source: International Labour Organization

▲ *The number of women in work as a percentage of the whole working population has not changed much.*

IN THEIR OWN WORDS

'My name is Youlya and I am 32. I work for a tour company – my job is challenging and very interesting. I organize many trips abroad and some trips around Russia. Foreign tourists are more educated today. They don't think any more that there are bears on the street and people in shell suits. The number of foreign tourists coming to this country and Russian tourists going abroad is increasing. What we need to do now is to develop better communications with other parts of Russia and build more good hotels in places of interest.'

Russians now have more money to spend on holidays. With their newly opened borders, Russian tourists have flocked to almost every part of the globe.

The number of foreign tourists visiting Russia fell dramatically after the collapse of the Soviet Union. Foreigners worried that Russia was unstable and dangerous, but they are now gradually returning. Tourists can now enjoy a much broader choice of holidays, from salmon fishing in Siberia to a trip into space!

► *Tourists enjoying a boat trip in St Petersburg.*

9 The Way Ahead

Much has changed in Russia and much more might change in the future. Russia still has a long way to go to reach prosperity. Pollution of the landscape might lead to climate change, while car use and industry are causing ever more damage to air and water quality. Natural resources are being widely and rapidly exploited and the population is shrinking.

However, there have also been many positive changes since the collapse of the Soviet Union. There are new freedoms for private companies and Russian consumers now get a much better deal. Apart from the Chechen conflict, Russia has largely avoided the political and civil conflicts that have been suffered in some other Eastern European countries. The government has survived a number of money crises and kept the economy going. Finances have also improved not only through economic growth, but also because more people are paying taxes.

During their history Russians have lived through many hardships, especially in the twentieth century. However, they remain energetic and resilient, positive and inventive, and are determined to make their country a good place to live.

▲ A future generation of music lovers plays on a monument to the famous composer Rachmaninov (1873–1943).

◄ The Internet is freely available and very popular with young Russians. Some 10 per cent of Russians are already regular Internet users and the number is steadily rising.

IN THEIR OWN WORDS

'My name is Alexander Tsvetayev. I am 17 years old and a pupil at a state high school. My favourite subjects are English language and maths. I spend most of my free time with my computer. After I leave school I want to go on to study Information Technology and become a computer programmer. I think life is improving in Russia – we just need more time and good government. I trust our government and think that our president is exactly what our country needs. We have problems, but I am sure that we can solve them in the near future.'

With its vast resources and highly educated post-Soviet population, Russia can look to the future with considerable hope. A lot remains to be done, but this is a country that has come a long way since it left the Soviet Union and has every chance of remaining a key country in the twenty-first century.

▼ *All these girls finished school with a gold medal for top marks in their year and now they are on their way to a ball organized by the mayor of Moscow.*

Glossary

Bolshevik A communist revolutionary group, led by Vladimir Lenin, that seized power in the 1917 Revolution in Russia.

Chechen conflict An ongoing war in the eastern part of north Caucasia in the south of Russia since the area declared itself independent in 1991.

Communism A theory and system of social and political organization in which property is owned by the community as a whole rather than by individuals.

Conscript Someone who has been required by the state to serve in the armed forces, rather than a volunteer or professional soldier.

Deforestation Cutting down trees for the timber industry or for fuel.

Ecology The study of the relationship of plants and animals to their physical and biological environment.

Economy A community's system of using its resources to produce wealth.

Emigration When people leave their own country and go to live in another country.

Hydroelectric power Electricity generated from turbines that are turned by the force of falling water.

Glasnost A policy of more openness and less secrecy introduced by Mikhail Gorbachev in the Soviet Union in the mid-1980s.

Greenhouse gases Gases in the atmosphere believed to trap heat from the Earth's surface and so contribute to global warming.

Immigration When people leave their own country and come to live in a new country.

Inflation A decline in the value of money in relation to the goods it can buy.

Kyoto Protocol An agreement signed in 1997 in Kyoto, Japan, which requires industrialized countries to reduce their emissions by 2012 to an average of 5 per cent below 1990 levels.

Market economy An economic system in which individuals, rather than the state, make decisions about what to produce and how to sell it, responding to what consumers want to buy.

National service A period of time during which young men are required by the state to serve in the armed forces.

NATO (North Atlantic Treaty Organization) An international organization established in 1949 to promote mutual defence and collective security that has been the primary Western military alliance since the Second World War.

Natural resources Mineral and other deposits formed by natural processes and available to be used by people.

Perestroika A policy of restructuring introduced by Mikhail Gorbachev to try to reform the Soviet Union in the mid-1980s.

Permafrost Permanently frozen subsoil.

Renewable energy Energy such as wind or wave power that can be used again and again, rather than fuels such as coal, which can only be burnt once.

Republic A state in which power belongs to the people, rather than to a royal family.

Soviet Union The state founded after the Russian Revolution, run by the communist party and made up of 15 republics. It covered one-sixth of the world's land surface, with a population of some 240 million.

Steppe Vast grassy plains.

Taiga The northern Russian and Siberian coniferous forest.

Thermal power sation A power station that is fuelled by oil, coal or gas.

Tsar The Russian king, or head of the Russian royal family.

World Heritage Site An area (or building) that possesses significant value for the whole of the world. Sites are selected by a United Nations committee.

Further Information

Sources

The Face of Russia: Anguish, Aspiration,
and Achievement in Russian Culture
by James H. Billington (TV Books Inc, 1999)

Lenin's Tomb – the last days of the
Soviet Empire
by David Remnick (Vintage Books, 1994)

Natasha's Dance – a cultural history of Russia
by Orlando Figes (Metropolitan Books, 2002)

Russia – a concise history
by Ronald Hingley (Thames & Hudson, 1991)

The Russian Chronicles – a thousand years that
changed the world
by Orlando Figes (ed.) *et al* (Thunder Bay
Press, 2001)

Further reading
Books to read
Step Into Russia (Heinemann Library, 1998)
Next Stop Russia (Heinemann Library, 1998)

For older readers
Russia 1991–2001 (Hodder Wayland, 2001)

Index

Page numbers in **bold** refer to photographs, maps or statistics panels.